Original title:
Whispers of the Wisteria

Copyright © 2025 Creative Arts Management OÜ
All rights reserved.

Author: Julian Prescott
ISBN HARDBACK: 978-1-80567-055-1
ISBN PAPERBACK: 978-1-80567-135-0

Beneath the Softness of Petal Dreams

Underneath the blooms that sway,
Bees are dancing, come what may.
A butterfly slips on a shoe,
Socks and sandals—what a view!

Petals tickle noses bright,
As critters scuffle left and right.
A squirrel steals a daisy crown,
While rabbits hop, they tumble down.

Insects tap to nature's beat,
Chasing shadows, oh so sweet.
A frog croaks jokes about the sun,
With laughter shared, the day is done.

The Ballet of Beasts in the Fragrant Shade

In the garden, where sprites play,
A hedgehog twirls in grand ballet.
A raccoon taps an old worn drum,
While all the flowers hum, oh hum!

A cat in a top hat prances round,
As crickets join with joyful sound.
A dance-off starts, who's got the flair?
Even the ants, they stop and stare.

A giraffe sneezes, leaves take flight,
'Tis a wonder, what a sight!
Mice slip slide in tiny shoes,
Chasing dreams beneath the hues.

Harmony in the Hush of Blooming Night

As twilight spreads its velvet cloak,
The toads have gathered for a joke.
Fireflies flash like tiny lights,
Making laughter on starry nights.

A hedgehog serenades the moon,
With a tune that ends too soon.
Crickets chirp their silly song,
While shadows dance the whole night long.

Whiskers twitch, and tails entwine,
A sleepy owl sips on some wine.
The night is full of playful cheer,
Where giggles drift and joy is near.

Beneath the Lavender Veil

Underneath the soft azure,
Bumblebees tease, it's pure allure.
A ladybug in polka dots,
Sips on nectar in happy spots.

A wise old owl gives advice,
"Don't be late—it's dinner nice!"
A hedgehog waits with a fork and knife,
"Where's my salad? It's dinner life!"

The daisies chuckle, the roses grin,
A picnic starts, let the fun begin.
As petals flutter, laughter sways,
In the garden, oh what days!

A Journey in the Sway of Petals

In gardens where giggles take flight,
Petals dance under moonlight bright.
Bumblebees don tiny hats,
While flowers trade jokes with chitchat.

A squirrel with flair, struts on a twig,
Claiming the crown, oh-so-dig!
With acorns as snacks, they laugh and prance,
In this quirky, nature-bound romance.

Look! A butterfly's done a somersault,
Winding through blooms, it's no fault!
While the roses roll their eyes,
At petals in a hula-hoop surprise!

So come, take a stroll in this silly space,
Where each little flower has a funny face.
Join the antics, share a grin,
In this land where giggles begin.

Following the Path of Lavender Hues

Through fields where lavender waves hello,
Chasing butterflies that move too slow.
A snail in sunglasses takes the lead,
As frogs insist on croaking their creed.

Bees buzz in rhythm, a tiny parade,
While daisies gossip, unafraid.
The sunflowers grin, tall and proud,
Waving to folks, drawing in a crowd.

A hedgehog hosts a tea party soon,
With thimble-sized cups beneath the moon.
Lavender cakes and honey sweet,
As critters gather for this tasty treat.

So waddle along this fragrant lane,
Where laughter reigns in sunshine or rain.
In this whimsical world, joy's the cue,
With lavender dreams in a giggling hue.

Murmurs of the Twilit Canopy

Underneath the dancing leaves,
A squirrel juggles acorn dreams.
The moonlight spills like melted cheese,
As fireflies plot their silly schemes.

A breeze tickles the branches high,
While crickets break into a jig.
The stars join in, twinkling shy,
A night so sweet, it makes you gig.

The owls hoot in a baffled tone,
Wondering where their snacks have flown.
Each shadow laughs, a silly bone,
In twilight's grasp, they're never alone.

With every chuckle soft and bright,
Nature's humor takes the stage.
In this strange, delightful night,
The forest plays as our own page.

The Soft Touch of Nature's Lullaby

Petals dance on a gentle breeze,
The bees are buzzing, making bees.
A sleepy frog begins to snore,
As daisies argue about the floor.

Butterflies are taking bets,
On who can land on the biggest net.
A dandelion puffs with glee,
While ants joke about their tea spree.

Clouds giggle, shifting shapes in tune,
While crickets croon beneath the moon.
Nature hums a silly song,
Its playful spirit, brave and strong.

With gnarled roots that twist and twine,
Each moment glimmers, truly fine.
Laughter floats on air so sweet,
A comedy of blooms and feats.

Emptiness Between the Blooms

In a garden where the petals spin,
A lazy turtle grins, takes in.
Empty pots await the rain,
While jumbled weeds beg for a train.

Behind each flower, tales unfold,
Of garden gnomes who've lost their gold.
The butterflies, in confused flight,
Switch partners mid-blossom, what a sight!

A stubborn snail won't hurry up,
While sipping on his morning cup.
Gossip whispers on the breeze,
Nature's chaos, sure to tease.

In every nook, a secret waits,
As nature laughs and plays with fate.
In emptiness, a punchline looms,
Among the giggles and the blooms.

Chasing Shadows in Blooming Dusk

At dusk, the shadows start to play,
Chasing crickets on their way.
Bouncing daisies hide and seek,
While ferns tease softly, not a peak.

A playful breeze sends petals twirling,
As evening whispers, gently swirling.
The robins tease with whistling tunes,
While bunnies hop beneath the moons.

Chasing giggles, a raccoon leaps,
Through blooms and bushes, over heaps.
Everyone's caught in nature's game,
In this funny little dance, no one's lame.

Against the twilight, laughter glows,
As joy in every corner flows.
In blooming dusk, the funny rush,
As shadows twirl and creatures hush.

Embraced by the Lush Surroundings

In a garden so bright, bees dance with glee,
They tease all the flowers, so carefree.
A squirrel drops nuts with a cheeky grin,
While the grass giggles softly, tickling their kin.

Beneath the large tree, a frog sings a tune,
A blue jay cackles, claiming the moon.
Snails plan a race, slow but with pride,
While the daisies all nod, can't hide their wide stride.

Butterflies flutter, wearing bright attire,
Spreading the joy, like a chorus in choir.
Each leaf has a tale, a secret to share,
As shadows hop around without any care.

Nature's a jester with tricks up her sleeve,
With giggles and chuckles that never deceive.
In a realm where laughter sprinkles the air,
Life dances in rhythm, it's a splendid affair.

Stillness of the Petals' Secrets

Raindrops hold secrets, a hush, then a splash,
Petals giggle lightly, as puddles all dash.
A ladybug winks, 'I'm the star of the show!'
While ants troop in lines, wearing glittering bow.

In shadows they hold a debate oh so grand,
About which flower is the best in the land.
The roses complain they're not getting their due,
While lilacs just laugh, 'We are prettier too!'

Mice hold a feast on the soft velvet grass,
In a tiny banquet, where all critters pass.
The mushrooms emerge, all dotted and wild,
Exchanging sweet gossip in full harmony, mild.

With laughter as nectar, the world spins so fine,
In gardens of giggles, where joy intertwines.
Every rustle a chuckle, and every breeze,
Carries tales of delight, a playful tease.

In the Arms of Gorgeous Tendrils

Vines twist and turn, a tangled ballet,
Where squirrels prepare for a nutty buffet.
Caterpillars plot their ascent to the sky,
While blooms, in their colors, wink slyly nearby.

Inchworms take bets on the speed of their crawl,
While chubby bumblebees bounce, having a ball.
A braver young flower dares tickle the breeze,
And the butterflies giggle, shivering with ease.

Tendrils wrap 'round, a soft nature's embrace,
While frogs shout out jokes with a charming grace.
"Why did the flower never get a date?
Too busy being bold, it was really first-rate!

A Caress of Nature's Breath

The wind tells a story through branches that sway,
As clouds roll by, playing hide and seek play.
Laughter erupts from a trapped bumblebee,
As petals shake wildly, such pure jubilee!

The sun throws a party, all creatures invite,
With cupcakes of dew, what a glorious sight!
Grasshoppers dance, in a jitterbug cheer,
While daisies bloom brighter, as summertime's here.

A playful raccoon sneaks a sip from the pond,
His splash makes the lilies respond with a bond.
Together they giggle, this sweet merry crew,
Creating a tapestry drenched in life's hue.

So join in the frolic, let laughter release,
'Neath the leafy embrace, you'll find your heart's peace.
In nature's fine clutches, where whimsy runs deep,
Every moment a joy, where spirits can leap.

Songs of the Gentle Drift

Beneath the trees, a giggle grows,
The flowers sway, in breezy clothes.
A squirrel dances, quite a sight,
In a top hat, chasing light.

A butterfly, with too much flair,
Tried to jump but lost mid-air.
The bees are buzzing, what a show,
In their tiny suits, they steal the flow.

A raccoon plays a slippery game,
Thinking he's stealthy, but oh, what shame!
He tips a pot, little ears perked,
Making the whole garden smirk.

In this garden, laughter spreads,
With every leaf that softly treads.
Nature chuckles, a merry tune,
Underneath the lazy moon.

The Veil of Amethyst Secrets

Violet blooms with cheeky grins,
Whispering tales of garden sins.
A chipmunk steals the snack parade,
Odyssey of crumbs, he won't evade.

Oh, the lilies, they roll their eyes,
When pigeons pitch their pizza flies.
A frog croaks in a deep bass voice,
Singing bad tunes, oh what a choice!

The breeze giggles, rustles leaves,
Telling stories of mischief thieves.
Daisies nod as the sun grows bold,
In a game of "who steals gold?"

With each petal, laughter brews,
In colors bright, a joyful muse.
The secrets bloom, loud and free,
In this garden jubilee.

A Hidden Dance of Color

Amidst the hues, a party's thrown,
Where daisies dance, their roots well known.
A clumsy bee, with pollen slack,
Trips on petals, oh, what a whack!

Fluffy clouds bring ballooning fun,
A baby rabbit tries to run.
He hops and flops, a silly spree,
Landing headfirst in a tub of pea!

The tulips giggle, swaying tall,
While ants march in their marching ball.
A ladder made of flowering vines,
As friendship's secret hopefully shines.

Under the sun, colors ignite,
With rainbows dancing in pure delight.
Nature's laughter holds the key,
To a world so wild and free.

When Serenity Blooms in Silence

In hush of petals, jokes take flight,
A snail claims he can run tonight.
But with a blink, he's on his way,
Carrying home, a leaf buffet!

The daisies giggle, can't contain,
As the sun drops like a silly stain.
A ladybug dressed up for tea,
But swirls around, unable to see!

Under the stars, the fireflies play,
Telling secrets at the end of the day.
Each twinkle, a wink from the sky,
While squirrels debate, who will fly high?

So hush, oh garden, with laughter clear,
The sounds of silence are all we hear.
With every bloom, brings a chuckle mild,
In this sweet sanctuary, forever wild.

Timeless Tales of the Swinging Vines

In gardens lush, the laughter grows,
With dancing leaves that tickle toes.
The vines confide their silly schemes,
While squirrels plot their nutty dreams.

A ladybug in polka dots,
Claims she's the queen of garden plots.
With swagger bold, she struts about,
While gnomes just stand and twitch in doubt.

The bumblebees wear tiny ties,
As they debate the sky and pies.
One thinks he's Shakespeare, oh so smart,
Yet all he writes is honey art.

Amidst the blooms, pup dares to bark,
Disturbing peace until it's dark.
The vines just giggle in the breeze,
As petals sway and shake with ease.

A Soft Serenade Among the Shadows

A nightingale sings quite off-key,
While shadows dance for all to see.
A raccoon joins with clumsy grace,
As moonlight paints a wobbly face.

The shadows jest, they tease the trees,
A game of tag in gentle breeze.
A firefly's light twinkles with glee,
While raccoons hold their own jamboree.

A cat rolls by, giving a yawn,
Declaring 'I'm the star of dawn!'
The leaves just chuckle, soft and low,
As breezes kiss them to and fro.

Oh, in this night, with laughter shared,
The creatures know they're truly cared.
Each giggle echoes in the dark,
As shadows play their joyful lark.

Beauty Through the Haze of Evening

The sunset blushes, skies ignite,
As butterflies prepare for flight.
They sip on nectar, giggling loud,
In dresses bright, they're quite a crowd.

The hedgehogs roll, a quirky sight,
In twilight's charm, a wobbly flight.
They navigate the blooms with cheer,
Pretending they are astronauts here.

The vines loop high, a playful tease,
As crickets form a jazzed-up spree.
With sounds so sweet, they dance along,
In the enchanted glow of dusk's song.

While fireflies flare like stars on ground,
The garden bursts with silly sound.
An evening's charm, so full of glee,
A magical maze of pure esprit.

Blooms that Breathe Beneath the Moon

Beneath the moon, the flowers sway,
In shadows, they invent their play.
A sunflower spins, a disco queen,
While daisies join the moonlit scene.

A toad leaps high, he thinks he's grand,
Declaring he will lead the band.
The petals blush, they can't contain,
Their laughter bubbling like champagne.

The night unfurls a fragrant sigh,
As crickets chirp, their songs fly high.
A bumblebee dons shades so sleek,
He winks and nods, playing the chic.

In blooms that breathe the night so sweet,
All nature joins in rhythmic beat.
The moon looks down, a jovial guest,
As petals dance, they feel so blessed.

The Murmurs Beneath Violet Clouds

Beneath the violets, a secret thrives,
Where squirrels share jokes with the buzzing hives.
A raccoon's opinion on pizza's the best,
He claims with a grin, it's a culinary quest.

Laughter dances with butterflies' wings,
As frogs debate over who softly sings.
Even the wind joins in with a sigh,
"Why is the moon always so shy?" they cry.

The daisies giggle, the tulips inquire,
"Who stole our sunlight? The sun's a liar!"
With each little chuckle, the garden comes alive,
In this silly realm, everyone can thrive.

As shadows play hide-and-seek between trees,
And the birds hold a gossip amongst the breeze.
Each petal is chuckling, all worries tossed,
In a world of giggles, no joy is lost.

Lush Canopy and Tender Thoughts

In the lush green heights, some birds begin,
A debate on who can wear the best grin.
The chipmunks jot notes on comedy shows,
While the owl just hoots, "I'm wise, don't you know?"

A raccoon in pajamas has taken a seat,
Sipping on nectar, it's quite the sweet treat.
He spills a few tales of his midnight raids,
While the fireflies blink as if cutting parades.

The vines twist and turn, telling jokes out loud,
While the daisies form a soft, giggling crowd.
"Why don't we bid for the softest of beds?"
Says the mossy old rock, with a nod of his head.

These moments of laughter in foliage spread,
Lift spirits like daisies, as sunshine is shed.
With banter around, none ever feel haste,
In this comedic haven, no moment's a waste.

Reverberations Among the Glistening Leaves

Leaves tremble with laughter as breezes rush by,
In shadows where creatures all join in the try.
The wise old tortoise, with wisdom quite vast,
Tells of yesteryears in a voice built to last.

The butterflies giggle, as they flit and fly,
Become comedians, zooming high in the sky.
"Why did the flower fail its big test?"
Cherubs chirp, "It forgot phone numbers, the jest!"

The brook chuckles loud as it tiptoes along,
While frogs play the chorus in a silly song.
All say, "Who needs scripts when nature can play?"
Join in, have some fun, let's brighten the day!

In moments like these, when sunshine is bright,
And laughter becomes a soft, playful light.
Every shimmer of leaf holds a tale so sweet,
In this vibrant retreat, life dances on feet.

Symphony of the Nightshade

Underneath the stars, a gathering of glee,
Where the critters hold court, you'll find them with tea.
A hedgehog's reciting some very old lore,
While the crickets provide the rhythm encore.

Moonlight is humor, it twinkles and shines,
The fireflies hold flashbacks of old olden times.
"Ever heard the one about branches that bend?"
Asked the owl, as snickers around him blend.

From shadows a fox tells a tale with some flair,
About missing socks and vegetable care.
The bunnies all chuckle, they can barely sit,
For the wildest of stories come out with a wit.

With these nightly musings beneath the bright sky,
The humor of nature is never too shy.
Each note shared with laughter is bound to unite,
In this symphony spun by the warmth of the night.

Love Letters Hidden in the Leaves

In the garden where giggles bloom,
I found a note, in a flower's room.
It said, 'Dear Bee, you make me buzz!'
But wait, it's signed from a clumsy fuzz!

The ants read it, and started to laugh,
They can't believe, it's a flowery gaffe.
'Your pollen's sweet, but your dance is clumsy,'
Said the ladybug, feeling quite sassy!

Underneath the lilac's sway,
Squirrels chatter about love's display.
But who knew a leaf could hide such a jest?
Nature's romance is truly the best!

So if you stroll through the green today,
Look for the letters that nature will play.
Because love's not serious, but rather a tease,
In a dress made of leaves, with a smile on the breeze!

Dance of the Lilac Breezes

The wind jumped in, with a giggling shout,
The lilacs swayed, round and about.
'Twist and twirl, just don't trip,
Or you'll end up in a rose bush's grip!'

The colors swirled like a carnival ride,
Butterflies joined, with grace and pride.
'Watch your step!' cried a bee with a grin,
'No falling here – we're trying to spin!'

A fox joined in, with his bushy tail,
Twirled the petals, without fail.
He slipped on a daisy and landed with flair,
As flowers giggled, floating in the air!

So let's dance with the lilacs tonight,
Where blooms are wild, and everything's bright.
With laughter as sweet as nectar divine,
We'll sway in joy, together, entwined!

The Scent of Unspoken Dreams

In the breeze where thoughts float free,
Dreams smell like cake, but where's the tea?
A squirrel dreams of acorns galore,
While a butterfly aims for open doors!

The daisies plot a secret surprise,
Whispers of cookies in sunbeam skies.
While clouds fluff up like fussy chef hats,
It's hard to think when you're chasing chats!

Beneath the boughs where shadows play,
Mice scribble hopes on a leaf bouquet.
But when they peek, the dreams all run,
'Catch us if you can, this is too fun!'

So breathe in deep, feast on the air,
Dreams frolic about, without a care.
For in the garden of laughter and schemes,
The scent of joy is the heart of dreams!

Petals and Poetry in the Soft Breeze

Petals dance, like they've lost their way,
Twirling to a rhythm, of giggles at play.
A daffodil scribbles a silly rhyme,
While bees keep the beat, buzzing in time!

A tulip dressed up, tried to impress,
But tripped on a peony, what a mess!
They laughed in the sunlight, so warm and bright,
Turning flops into quotes, in sheer delight!

The breeze plays a tune, a fluttering sound,
As two daisies do cartwheels upon the ground.
Whirling their stories, a verse or a shout,
Creating a poem, when the world's turned out!

In this garden where petals and poetry meet,
Life's silly moments are perfectly sweet.
So let's toss our cares in the blooming air,
Join the laughter, friend, if you dare!

Secrets of the Twilit Arbor

In twilight's blush, trees start to giggle,
While shadows dance and leaves do wiggle.
A squirrel in a bowtie, eating a tart,
Proclaims he's the king, with a very full heart.

A raccoon with a grin, swipes a picnic feast,
He brings out the tools, but he's really a beast.
The moonlight sparkles, they laugh 'til they drop,
As acorns rain down, they call for a mop.

Beneath the stars, secrets fit like a glove,
With wisecracks and snacks, they all rise above.
A dance through the night till breakfast is near,
They toast with their cups, full of berry light beer.

So come take a stroll where the witties roam free,
Where jokes fill the air like a sweet honeybee.
In the arbor of fun, where stories combine,
You'll find laughter's haven, a true friend of mine.

Celestial Whispers in Blooming Time

When blossoms start to giggle in the sun,
Bees wear tiny hats as they're having fun.
A daisy dons sunglasses, ready to shine,
While tulips take selfies, sipping on wine.

The lavender sings, in a high-pitched tone,
With fashion-forward petals they just have grown.
Even vines wear their shorts, quite the bold style,
As daisies crack jokes, making all of us smile.

A breeze brings confetti, from petals up high,
As blades of grass cheer, waving 'hi' to the sky.
Hummingbirds jitterbug, with moves so extreme,
While nature throws parties, like it's all a big dream.

So if you hear giggles in colorful bloom,
Join in on the laughter, dispel any gloom.
In gardens of joy, play your favorite rhyme,
Among the sweet chaos, in blooming time.

Night's Embrace on Pink Petal Pathways

Under the stars, petals play hide-and-seek,
While crickets perform their odd little squeak.
Fireflies don top hats, they flicker and prance,
Inviting the moon to a whimsical dance.

The breeze plays guitar, but has two left feet,
While owls hoot a rhythm that's pretty offbeat.
Nestled in petals, a raccoon starts a show,
Telling tall tales of the junk food he knows.

Night's embrace is warm as it tucks in the dew,
While daisies chuckle at the stars' silly hue.
A party of shadows makes night feel alive,
With everyone dancing, it's hard to survive!

So if you hear laughter from paths painted pink,
Join in the fun; don't you dare even blink.
Under the moonlight, let troubles be few,
In this riotous night where joy feels so new!

Wistful Thoughts on a Gentle Breeze

A dandelion's whisper floats up to the sky,
While butterflies giggle, asking 'Oh my!'.
With curious clouds playing games, soft and free,
They pen their own stories on pages of glee.

Tulips gossip with roses, trading their tales,
As a squirrel tells secrets through playful exhales.
Unicorns prance by on a whimsy-topped ship,
Waving to daisies, who cheer with each skip.

A breeze hums a tune, just a tad off the mark,
While shadows join in, creating a spark.
In the land of the silly, where giggles take flight,
Where thoughts swirl around like a disco ball's light.

So catch the soft laughter on the whimsy-filled air,
Embrace the delight that's unexpected, yet rare.
For in this sweet moment, let your spirit tease,
And dance with the daydreams on a gentle breeze.

Secret Murmurs of the Blossoming Vines

In the garden, giggles bloom,
A bee lost, caught in a loom.
Petals playing hide and seek,
Nature's jesters, quite unique.

A squirrel schemes on a sweet spree,
Stealing snacks from a nearby tree.
"Oh no!" the birdies chirp in shock,
As acorns tumble, tick tock, tick tock.

The flowers gossip, bloomers on strike,
Trading secrets like kids on a bike.
"Who wore what?" they curiously ask,
While butterflies don their fancy mask.

Dancing shadows in the sun's light,
A piñata burst, a sheer delight.
With petals raining down like cheer,
The garden's laughter is crystal clear.

Lament of the Violet Canopy

Beneath the purples, giggles hide,
A caterpillar slipped, what a ride!
"Is this my fate?" he wished to know,
In the petals, faces start to glow.

A turtle stumbled, lost his way,
Round and round, he'd laugh and sway.
"Hey there, slowpoke!" a robin mocked,
As the violets cheered, unblocked.

The breezes danced, tails up in jest,
While flowers swayed, giving their best.
"Join the fun!" the daisies cried,
As laughter echoed, far and wide.

"Why so serious?" the lilies teased,
As bees zoomed by, humor never ceased.
In this canopy of goofy tones,
Nature's smiles are softly honed.

Tales Beneath the Lavender Shelter

Beneath the lavender, tales take flight,
Where crickets laugh late into the night.
A ladybug slips on a leaf,
"Oh dear!" she gasps, missing belief.

The rabbits giggle at their own chase,
In lavender fields, a silly race.
"I'm faster!" one bounces, proud of his feat,
While daisies cheer, tapping their feet.

Now a hedgehog joins in the fun,
Rolling down hills, oh, what a run!
"Not again!" the flowers say with glee,
As they scatter with laughter, wild and free.

The nightingale sings a tune so bright,
As insects clap under the moonlight.
Together they weave a whimsical dream,
While shadows dance, a giggling team.

Echoes of the Cascading Blooms

In the rush of blooms, laughter flows,
Petal parties, where no one knows.
"What's that?" a bumblebee huffs and puffs,
As roses giggle, playing tough.

The winds carry tales of a bloom so rare,
"I swear it just smirked!" says a jaunty hare.
Daisies gossip with every sway,
Spreading humor on a sunny day.

A chubby snail, so proud, he glides,
In a daffodil cup, where mischief hides.
"Fancy a ride?" the flowers tease,
As he wiggles and jiggles with utmost ease.

At dusk, the glowworms join the fray,
Illuminating silliness in a playful way.
Echoes of laughter, a garden so bright,
As blooms break into dance, a joyful sight.

Dances among the Delicate Petals

Beneath the blooms, the squirrels play,
They twirl and leap in bright ballet.
A bee buzzes in, a huge ballet fan,
Just don't let him land on your hand!

The petals drop like confetti rain,
A dance party for the bug brigade.
Bees in tuxedos, ants in a line,
This garden's nuts—we're having a time!

A ladybug spins with all her might,
While grasshoppers hop, oh what a sight!
Butterflies flutter, wearing their best,
Oh dear, is everyone ready for the nest?

With petals falling, laughter's the key,
Every bloom holds a secret spree.
Join the fun, let the petals be,
We're all a little silly, can't you see?

The Lure of the Lilac Breeze

The lilac sways in the breezy gust,
A dance of scents that we all trust.
A couple a-chasing with giggly glee,
Oops! Watch out for that bumblebee!

With every sniff, a chuckle loud,
A whiff of mischief from the crowd.
The trees all sway, they seem amused,
As flower petals whisper and get confused.

A dog runs past with a silly bark,
Chasing a butterfly, oh what a lark!
The breeze carries tales of pranks in bloom,
Where every petal lands is a little room.

So laugh along with the little things,
The joy that every springtime brings.
In this lilac realm of playful tease,
The breeze will tickle, it aims to please!

Secrets Linger in the Twilight

When twilight falls upon the lawn,
The fireflies flash—come on, respond!
There's gossip buzzing in the night,
While stars giggle at the silly sight.

A toad croaks jokes in a croaky voice,
The crickets chirp, oh what a choice!
Under a moonbeam, secrets play,
While shadows dance and gleefully sway.

The hedgehog snorts with a cartwheel twist,
In a secret game, he can't resist.
A raccoon peeks, made a funny face,
While night blooms chuckle—it's quite the place!

So gather round by soft moonlight,
With laughter spilling, it feels just right.
In twilight's arms, let fun abide,
For secrets linger where joy won't hide!

Embrace of the Hanging Blossoms

In the garden where plants like to sway,
Hanging blooms join in every play.
A rabbit hops, his ears in flight,
Trying to dodge those blossoms' might!

Daring blooms dance with every breeze,
While worms wiggle, looking for cheese.
Blossoms giggle, sway a little slow,
As insects march in a cheery row.

A climber's trap, it's such a sight,
As kids swing from blossoms with all their might.
Laughing petals drop with flair,
"Catch me if you can!"—no burden, no care.

So let us sway in the springtime breeze,
Amongst the petals, we'll do as we please.
In the embrace of blooms, laughter's our song,
In this garden haven, come sing along!

Tranquil Echoes Under Stars

In a garden where giggles play,
The moon winks bright, come what may.
Bubbly blooms dance to a tune,
While frogs croak jokes beneath the moon.

A cat in a hat struts with flair,
He stops to twirl in the cool night air.
The daisies chuckle, petals unfurl,
As fireflies join the whimsical swirl.

Stars tease the clouds, their fluffy crew,
While crickets chirp their take on the blue.
Every leaf rustles with playful glee,
In this nighttime realm, wild and free.

Laughter hangs on the breeze so light,
As gardens erupt in pure delight.
With echoes of joy, the night feels right,
Under the stars, what a funny sight!

Tales from Under a Violet Sky

Under a sky brushed with violet hue,
A jester prances, his antics ensue.
With a quirk and a twirl, he shakes the night,
Chasing the shadows, pretty and bright.

A friendly raccoon dons a small crown,
Claiming the throne as he dances around.
The daisies giggle, the lilies sing,
To this royal ball, what joy they bring!

Squirrels tell tales, all tangled and fun,
Of a lost acorn, they ran 'til they spun.
Hilarity grows like a flower in bloom,
In this merry gathering, there's never gloom!

Beneath the indigo, wishes take flight,
With tittering tones floating into the night.
Laughter is sewn through foliage's seams,
In a magical garden stitched from dreams.

Delicate Lullabies in the Dark

Amidst shadows, a chorus is born,
A lullaby sung by a light-hearted morn.
Tiny insects join in with a buzz,
Creating a symphony, just because.

A sleepy hedgehog hums to the beat,
While crickets provide a tap with their feet.
The night blooms giggle, their smell so sweet,
As fireflies flicker, like stars they greet.

Rustling leaves share secrets and rhymes,
Tickling the air as they sway through the times.
With a wink and a grin, the night unfolds,
Laughter wrapped in dreams, gently told.

Under the moon's playful gaze,
New stories arise in delightful array.
So join in the fun, let your spirit embark,
To sing the soft tunes that echo in the dark!

Serenity Woven in Floral Whispers

In a patch of cheer where the flowers jest,
Bees in bowties buzz with zest.
A butterfly's flutter, a giggling spree,
Brings smiles to blooms, oh what glee!

With petals like pages, tales intertwine,
A sunflower reads its punchline divine.
Buds chuckle softly, teasing the breeze,
In this floral fiesta, nature aims to please.

Under the shade where the grass tickles toes,
A dance of the daisies, where laughter flows.
Jolly old trees join in the fun,
In a comedy show 'til the day is done.

As twilight drapes in hues so bright,
With laughter echoing, hearts take flight.
It's a serenade from the blooms to the world,
In this garden of joy, where magic is twirled!

Sweet Cadence of Fading Colors

Fuchsia socks on a breeze,
Bright green hat stealing cheese,
Daisies giggle, hats they pluck,
A dance of hues, a stroke of luck.

Lavender winks, plays peek-a-boo,
Sunflowers join, it's quite a crew,
They paint the sky a silly hue,
While butterflies laugh, just passing through.

Crickets hum in a jazzy style,
Buttercups prance, it's quite a mile,
Marigolds sport a tiny crown,
As colors fade, they never frown.

In this garden, humor's loud,
Petals chuckle, oh so proud,
Nature's jesters, never shy,
Making us laugh until we cry.

The Enigma of Blooms in Bloom

Tulips twist, they can't decide,
To be bold or run and hide,
Dandelions don their capes,
In superhero forms, they escape.

Bumblebees sporting tiny shades,
Buzz along in comical parades,
Carnations plotting silly schemes,
As daisies chase their wildest dreams.

Pansies whisper jokes on leaves,
About the quirks that spring deceives,
They giggle soft in colors bright,
Under a moon of laughter light.

A rose told a joke, it went too far,
But laughter bloomed, like a shooting star,
Each petal holds a secret joke,
In the garden where whimsy spoke.

Gentle Reveries of the Silken Bower

Vines entwined, forming a couch,
Where snails play chess, and mice can vouch,
With laughter echoing in the air,
As frogs strut by without a care.

Butterflies rumors spread, oh dear,
"Did you hear what's blooming here?"
Jasmine smells, tickles the nose,
As teasels gossip, where no one goes.

Inside the bower, tales unfold,
Of flowers brave and stories bold,
With petals blushing, they can't resist,
To join in on the humor list.

Roses wink at a passing bee,
Who fluffs his coat and shouts with glee,
The bower dances, full of cheer,
With nature's giggles ringing clear.

The Quiet Lullaby of Blossoming Vines

In the shade where the shadows play,
Vines weave tales at the end of day,
With leaves that flutter, news unfolds,
Of silly spouts and jovial molds.

A chubby caterpillar steals the show,
Wiggling through shrubbery, nice and slow,
Chasing a ladybug, all in fun,
While crickets chirp, "You've just begun!"

Petunia shared her candy stash,
While sweet peas giggled and made a splash,
The wind hummed soft, a lullaby,
As flowers twirled, reaching for the sky.

Underneath the weave of green,
Laughter sprang from a hidden scene,
In every breeze, a silly line,
Amidst the vines, where laughter shines.

The Melody of Swaying Petals

In the garden, petals dance,
They twirl around without a chance.
A breeze comes in, they sway and shout,
"Hold on tight, don't fall out!"

Bumbles buzz on silly flights,
Chasing dreams through sunny heights.
One flew right into a pie,
"Oops! I wanted blueberry!" he cried.

Lazy bees take afternoon naps,
While silly squirrels play silly traps.
They steal the flowers for their hats,
"Fashion first! Go home, dear cats!"

Dancing blooms just laugh and tease,
They sway along with playful ease.
In this garden, humor grows,
Even petals know how it flows.

Tales Beneath the Cascading Vines

Beneath the vines, where laughter hides,
The bunnies hop with fashion strides.
They wear sunglasses, looking grand,
And strike a pose – isn't it bland?

A squirrel tells stories of his finds,
Nuts and leaves, he cleverly binds.
"I'm a chef! Try my nutty stew!"
"We'll stick to grass, thank you!"

The flowers gossip, it's quite a scene,
Spinning tales that weren't quite clean.
"Did you see that butterfly fall?"
"Yes! He thought he was nothing at all!"

Beneath these vines, life's a hoot,
With every leaf, a silly root.
Nature laughs, not a care to feign,
In their antics, joy remains.

Fragile Threads of Nature's Heart

Threads of green weave tales so fine,
Nature chuckles over a glass of wine.
"Hey, leaf! Don't you lose your grip!"
"Not a chance, I love this trip!"

Tiny critters play peek-a-boo,
With every rustle, they plot anew.
A roly-poly thinks he's a king,
"Bow to me! I can do anything!"

Petal gossip sparkles in the sun,
"Did you see that bee? He's on the run!"
With tea parties and cakes so sweet,
The whole garden joins for a funny treat.

Fragile threads, yet stories bold,
Nature's comedy never gets old.
With every giggle, the heart takes flight,
In the dance of petals, all feels right.

Candlelight and Floral Whispers

In candlelight, dreams flutter fast,
While flowers gossip of the past.
"Remember when he tripped on roots?"
"Oh yes! He blushed just like our fruits!"

The daisies host a tea affair,
With buttercups as ladies fair.
"Pass the sugar, hold the cream,
It's time to laugh, or so it seems!"

Violets play piano tunes,
That make the bumblebees dance as loons.
"Let's have a party, let's spread cheer!
And don't forget the dancing deer!"

Amidst the glow, the humor drips,
With petals and laughter, life never slips.
In this garden, joy finds a lane,
With every candle, it's not in vain.

Languid Breezes and Colors Unfold

A breeze so lazy, makes me smile,
Petals drift by, with quite a style.
Colors dance like they're at a rave,
In the garden, feeling oh so brave.

The bees are buzzing, wearing shades,
While lazy frogs pretend to wade.
Even the daisies start to sway,
As if to say, 'Come dance and play!'

A cat on the fence, snoozing away,
Dreaming of fish that would never stray.
Nearby, a snail is in a race,
But just keeps failing, what a pace!

Each bloom giggles at a tiny joke,
Petals flapping like a sunlit cloak.
In this garden, laughter takes flight,
Where even shadows join in delight.

Reveries Among the Draped Blooms

Amongst the blooms, thoughts drift and sway,
A butterfly sneezes, oh what a day!
The tulips gossip, with petals aflutter,
While daisies plot pranks, their laughter a stutter.

A dandelion wished for a glamorous crown,
But the wind just giggled and blew it down.
It spun round and round, like a jolly old fool,
Wishing for fortune, yet stuck in a pool.

A squirrel in shades munches on seeds,
Chasing the shadows, fulfilling wild needs.
While willow branches sweep with flair,
It's a garden party, come if you dare!

Here life unfolds, with humor and cheer,
Nature's comedy, oh so sincere.
In blooms' embrace, we can just pretend,
That every petal is a fun-loving friend.

An Ode to the Swirling Petals

Oh petals, swirling in a merry dance,
Who knew the garden could offer this chance?
They tickle the air, like laughter so light,
Making the sun beam with sheer delight.

A bee plays the spoons, what a fine sound,
While ladybugs cheer, with legs off the ground.
"Catch me if you can!" the petals declare,
Like comets a-flying, without a care.

The roses huddle, sharing sweet jokes,
While hedgehogs listen, with pokey coax.
"Why did the flower refuse to play?
It couldn't find pollen, what a cliché!"

In swirling joy, the petal parade,
Making each moment a vibrant escapade.
Even the sun can't resist to partake,
As blossoms of laughter unite for the sake.

Shadows of the Twilight Garden

At twilight's hour, the shadows tease,
As crickets serenade the gentle breeze.
A mystery lingers, but who makes the noise?
The moon's just giggling with her lunar poise.

The roses whisper secrets in shades of red,
While ferns start playing hide and seek instead.
Each leaf holds a joke, some silly and sweet,
As bunnies hop by, their tiny hearts beat.

The lanterns blink, what a sight to behold,
While shadowy frogs tell tales, bold.
"Was that a ghost or just a lost cat?"
"More like a rumor, who could have spat?"

In this twilight garden, laughter soars high,
With every shadow, another sigh.
Here's to the moments, both quirky and bright,
Where shadows and petals share giggles at night.

Threads of Perfumed Memories

In a garden where giggles bloom,
Silly squirrels plot with a broom.
They dance on the breeze, oh what a show,
Chasing scents where the laughter flows.

Petals fall like confetti bright,
We giggle as they take flight.
A bee in a hat goes buzzing by,
With a bowtie on, oh my, oh my!

Each bloom winks with mischief near,
As carrots tell secrets, oh dear!
The daisies gossip, the pansies laugh,
While cacti draw maps on their graph.

In this chaos of blossoms and fun,
We let our spirits run and run.
With each petal that lands, a chuckle we share,
In memories made here, no room for despair.

Lament of the Grapevine Shadows

In the twilight where shadows prance,
A grapevine whispers to a chance.
Its tendrils twirl, a comical dance,
While the moon chuckles, giving a glance.

Oh, the grapes pair well with the night,
As they plot a mischief-filled flight.
They roll on the ground, causing a fuss,
As the fireflies blink and make a fuss.

A cluster of grapes, all in a row,
Scribbling jokes that only they know.
With laughter in vines, they swing and sway,
In the shadowy world where they play.

With giggles and jokes, the night unfolds,
While the stems tell tales that no one holds.
In whispers of merriment, silly yet wise,
The grapevines giggle under starry skies.

When Time Stands Still in Petal Rain

As petals drift down, oh what a sight,
Time stands still, and that's just right.
Caught in a loop of giggles and glee,
The best of the moment, just you and me.

Puddles form where the petals land,
Reflecting smiles, quite unplanned.
We jump in with splashes, like children so free,
Turning petals to boats for a whimsical spree.

And a cheeky butterfly decides to join,
Wings like a jester, ready to coin.
It flutters and dances with grace so grand,
While we laugh and sing, hand in hand.

Time may pause in this petal rain,
Yet our laughter echoes, an endless gain.
With each bloom that falls, our hearts take flight,
In the magical moment, all feels just right.

A Symphony of Twisting Tendrils

In a garden where tendrils intertwine,
A symphony plays, oh isn't it fine?
With each twist and jiggle, the vines take a bow,
As the crickets join in, what a row!

The roses hum loudly, no soft serenade,
While daisies tap dance, unafraid.
A trumpet of peonies leads the parade,
As laughter erupts, a delightful charade.

The violets sway to a jazzy beat,
As the shrubs strum chords with nimble feet.
Even the weeds join in the fun,
Making a ruckus till the day is done.

With giggles and gigabytes of glee,
The garden boasts its symphony.
A gathering of flora, a humorous thrill,
Where every leaf dances, and hearts are filled.

Moonlit Serenade Among the Petals

Beneath the moon so bright and round,
A squirrel danced, no grace was found.
The flowers giggled, swayed, and shook,
As he tripped over a hidden nook.

The bees hummed tunes, a buzzing band,
While blooms applauded, a floral stand.
A frog croaked out a silly tune,
Making petals sway, like a cartoon.

At midnight's hour, a breeze did sigh,
And fireflies lit the chatter high.
"Do we even need a stage?" they said,
As petals dreamt of royal bread.

So if you hear a laugh or two,
Know it's nature's comedy crew.
Underneath the softest night,
Petals party till morning light.

Hushed Secrets of the Twisting Branches

A raccoon claimed a twig, quite bold,
With stories only leaves had told.
The branches leaned in close, they grinned,
With secrets ripe, like fruit unpinned.

The owls hooted, oh what a jest,
"Who needs a show when we're the best?"
They blinked and winked, wise but sly,
As squirrels chuckled, "Just pass by!"

Through knots and knots of tangled cheer,
The wise old tree could almost hear.
A joke about a squirrel's hat,
That somehow landed on the brat.

With rustling leaves and playful sounds,
Nature's laughter knows no bounds.
Beneath the branches, tales unfold,
As nighttime's laughter turns to gold.

The Language of Flowers in Twilight

In twilight's glow, the daisies play,
They whisper tales, no one can say.
A dandelion sneezed, quite loud,
While roses bowed, so very proud.

Tulips rolled their eyes with flair,
"Did you just hear that? Oh, who dared?"
The violets giggled, couldn't hold,
As lilacs boasted tales retold.

A daisy claimed it knew a guy,
"A bumblebee with quite the tie!"
The peonies chimed, "What's this new trend?"
And laughter bloomed without an end.

So when you stroll through evening's charms,
Look close for flowers and their psalms.
For in the night, the petals jest,
In twilight's hush, they never rest.

Shadows Beneath the Flowering Veil

Under blossoms, secrets curl,
With laughter hiding, what a whirl!
A toad, a croaker, took the lead,
He told the tale of a lost seed.

The petals chuckled, swaying low,
"Who knows what else might steal the show?"
A butterfly flitted, laughed so bright,
Daring shadows to join the night.

A gopher popped up with a grin,
"Was it me or you? Now where've we been?"
All around, the blooms took note,
As nature's humor kept them afloat.

So linger here where laughter plays,
In nature's heart, where joy displays.
For underneath that floral veil,
Are tales and chuckles that never pale.

Secrets Drifting Through the Indigo Night

A frog croaks out a cheesy joke,
Beneath the stars, where shadows poke.
The moon smirks at the rustling leaves,
As crickets clap in their funny sleeves.

Atop the fence, a cat makes a leap,
Chasing dreams in shadows so deep.
A rabbit giggles, with a twinkle of glee,
Sure he's found the best hide and seek spree.

Bats play tag in a game of doubt,
Swapping tales that twist and pout.
A firefly stumbles in the air,
Telling secrets without a care.

The night wears on, filled with chatter,
Where silly tales are all that matter.
And in the end, they all declare,
Laughter's the brightest anywhere.

A Tapestry of Soft Voices

In the garden where colors collide,
Flowers gossip with petal-filled pride.
'Did you hear what Rose said today?'
'Oh, I can't wait to hear the play!'

Daisies giggle, as bees zoom by,
While tulips nod and lift their eye.
A daffodil's silly dance in the breeze,
Makes the whole patch bend with ease.

Marigolds burst with laughter and light,
In a symphony of joyous delight.
While violets plot mischief and cheer,
Saying, "Wait 'til the humans come near!"

A chorus of petals flicks and flutters,
As petals chat in vibrant stutters.
Whispers of joy spread out like a wave,
In nature's silly, colorful rave.

The Enchanted Garden's Silken Stories

Beneath a tree, a snail sings bright,
Of dreams spun in the moonlit night.
A ladybug sways with impeccable flair,
While a worm tells a tale of a funny scare.

Lilies splash laughter in the pond,
As fish jump high, quite the stunt!
A dragonfly twirls in a dizzy dance,
"We've got rhythm!" it shouts, taking a chance.

Bumblebees buzzing in jolly chorus,
Share secrets of who's the prettiest flora.
With every buzz and flip, they sing,
Bringing to life a joyful spring.

Comets of laughter sprinkle down,
In the realm of petals, there's no frown.
As tales unfold where the laughter plays,
In a magical garden that tickles all days.

Beneath the Canopy of Forget-Me-Nots

Beneath quiet blooms, stories abound,
Of a squirrel who wears a nutty crown.
He argues with a butterfly so bold,
'Your wings are pretty, but my tales are gold!'

A dandelion puffs with cheerful might,
Spreading wishes all through the night.
While creeping ivy joins the show,
'What's a vine gotta do to steal the glow?'

A pair of owls hoot with delight,
As they share riddles under the moonlight.
One hiccuped owl, with feathers so grand,
Fell off his perch, oh what a stand!

The canopy dances with chuckles and scoffs,
As shadows mingle and silence scoffs.
In every corner, joy does sprout,
In this place of laughter, there's no doubt.

Secrets in the Swaying Vines

Underneath the tangled leaves,
A squirrel stole my sandwich with ease.
He giggled and darted, such a tease,
While I pondered my fate, now a tease.

The vines sway gently, a breeze so sly,
A raccoon in pajamas drinks some chai.
They chuckle at humans passing by,
As I trip on roots, oh my, oh my!

In the shade, a rabbit does dance,
With moves that could charm, a funny romance.
He bows and sways, oh what a chance,
To join in the fun, take a stance!

The breeze hums tunes to all of us,
While bugs play a band, no need to fuss.
Nature's a stage without a bus,
In this leafy realm, we just adjust.

Echoes of Enchanted Blooms

Petals gossip like old friends,
While bees plan trips with no ends.
A dandelion wishes to mend,
His puffball woes as the laughter blends.

Fragrant flowers are quite the jest,
They bloom and giggle, never rest.
With pollen jokes, they feel so blessed,
While perfume puns swirl through the fest.

Among the petals, secrets spill,
As butterflies plot a comedy thrill.
The garden's alive with a funny chill,
Each bloom a player, with star power still.

Beneath the sun's warm-hearted glance,
A ladybug leads a waltz of chance.
With each tiny step, a wild prance,
In fields of laughter, they romance.

Serenade of the Scented Canopy

The vines giggle with a glint in their eyes,
As birds trade jokes from their lofty skies.
The petals sway with silly sighs,
Creating a chorus that never complies.

A lazy bee hums a tune just wrong,
While ants march by, a comedic throng.
They giggle and wriggle, feeling strong,
Each pollen pit-stop, never too long.

Blossoms tease the wandering breeze,
As branches tap dance with such ease.
A leaf in the air puts on quite a tease,
Playing tag with both laughter and cheese.

In this leafy theater full of grins,
The sun shares jokes, everyone spins.
A parade of petals, laughter begins,
In this fragrant world, joy always wins!

Moonlight and Mystic Twirls

Under the moon, the night takes flight,
As shadows dance and giggle in light.
The stars wink down with mischief bright,
While owls perform their comedy right.

The grass claims a worm as its friend,
It tells tales of soil, a twist to send.
With each squirm and slither, it does blend,
In laughter's embrace that will not end.

A swing from a branch, what a delight,
While crickets chirp, like stars of the night.
They sing with glee, a joke in flight,
As the moon beams down, a silver light.

Beneath these canopies, dreams entwine,
Comedic chaos, a twist in the vine.
With nature's own jokes, so divine,
The moonlight laughs, and all is fine.

Gossamer Dreams Under a Floral Arch

Beneath blooms so grand, they giggle and sway,
Dreams float like bubbles, then pop in dismay.
A bee in a tux, with a bow tie so neat,
Dances with petals, oh what a sweet treat.

The breeze has a chuckle, as leaves start to tease,
Telling tall tales to the honey-drenched bees.
A cat in a top hat struts grand on the scene,
Thinking he's royalty, oh what a routine!

Butterflies chuckle, in colors so bright,
While daisies gossip in pure morning light.
With laughter around, how can one feel blue?
Nature's a circus, and we're all in view!

So come to this haven, where mischief conducts,
We'll laugh with the blooms, and share all our quirks.
For in this lush garden, with giggles we play,
Life's just a frolic, let worries decay.

In the Garden of Sighs

In a garden where trees are too bored to stand,
They toss little leaves like cards from their hand.
A turtle in slippers takes life at his speed,
Stops by for a chat, it's polite indeed!

The roses complain, 'We're too sweet this year!'
While the lilies laugh loud, 'We don't shed a tear!'
Though the sun makes it hot, the humor is cool,
A gnome tells a joke, becomes the class fool.

The clouds loaf above, with no plans to unfold,
They giggle at runners, too frantic, too bold.
The daisies are plotting, a prank they will pull,
To tickle the toes of a passerby fool!

So if you should find, your mood's feeling gray,
Skip down to this garden, where laughter will play.
In this land of blunders, with smiles that shine bright,
Each sigh turns to giggle, oh, what pure delight!

The Language of Fading Fragrance

In a realm where scents speak, each flower has flair,
The lilacs declare, 'We're the best around here!'
Carnations roll eyes, 'Oh please, what a scene,'
While violets snicker, 'You're too loud, you green!'

The wind takes their words, like a gossiping friend,
Carrying whispers as messages send.
Each bloom has a tale, of fumbles and falls,
They try to outshine, but stumble in thralls.

Old herbs in the corner, they harken the past,
'We've been through tough times, oh they fly by so fast!'
The mint cracks a smile, 'We'll spice things anew,'
While roses snicker, 'That's old news, how true!'

But the air is a ruckus, a symphony sweet,
In the language of flora, we find joy complete.
So come take a whiff, let the fun be your guide,
In this fragrant fiesta, where laughter won't hide!

Twilight's Embrace in Indigo Hues

When twilight strolls in, with its indigo cloak,
The stars crack a joke, and the moon starts to poke.
Crickets in tuxedos begin their grand song,
They dance in the dark, but their rhythm's all wrong.

The hedgehogs are gossiping, ruffling their spines,
While fireflies wink, with luminous signs.
A raccoon in shades, with a snack just for fun,
Cracks up at the fireflies, who think they've won.

As shadows grow long, silliness reigns,
With owls perched high, sharing wise little refrains.
'Whooo's the comedian?' one sly feathered friend,
And everyone chuckles, this jest never ends.

So revel in dusk, where humor takes stage,
For laughter in twilight is all the right page.
In indigo hues, let the giggles take flight,
For a night full of joy, in the soft, silver light!

The Unseen Harmony Among the Vines

The vines conspire, plotting schemes,
They giggle softly, sharing dreams.
A caterpillar steals a glance,
While flowers join the wiggly dance.

A bee stings laughter, buzzes away,
The ladybug joins in the play.
"Is your name Bea-rilliant?" they tease,
As petals sway upon the breeze.

A bumblebee crafts an awkward line,
With clumsy moves, he thinks he's fine.
But tangled vines show no mercy,
"Don't trip, dear friend, it's a bit girly!"

Yet in this vine-tangled community,
The mishaps grow in unity.
From flower to flower, travels the jest,
Nature's humor is at its best.

Murmurs Beneath the Petaled Canopy

Underneath blooms, creatures conspire,
A snail jokes slowly about his attire.
"Why rush?" he says with a wink so sly,
While passing ants march, oh my, oh my!

A squirrel shimmies, gives a great laugh,
"Why don't you try a fun photograph?"
But the camera's lens just blinks and flares,
And the critters scatter, leaving their cares.

A bazaar of sounds, the petals sway,
As grasshoppers chirp a duet in play.
"Is it me, or does the sun seem shy?"
"Or perhaps it just wants a slice of pie?"

But in the shade, a wise owl grins,
"The jokes may stop when the twilight spins.
For all who gather beneath this dome,
Find laughter echoes, and this is home."

Secrets in the Twilight's Grasp

Twilight chuckles, the stars peek through,
"It's time for the night cap," a firefly flew.
With glow and giggles in every flick,
A moth jumped in, performing a trick!

"Why don't you let those wings be free?"
Said the cricket, hopping with glee.
"You've got the rhythm, let's dance the night,
We'll channel the mischief, make it right!"

Leaves shake with secrets, chuckles abound,
As shadows play and silliness surrounds.
"I don't mind thorns, if they make me laugh,
Even prickly plants can cut a path!"

But the moon peeks down, giggling too,
"Careful, my friends, don't get too askew!
For in this light, one's humor soars,
But in the morning, it's back to chores!"

Enchantment in Every Curl

Each curl of vine tells a silly tale,
Of a bug in love with a giant snail.
"Don't be shy, take her to the party!"
Said a bold little ant, feeling so hearty.

The petals blush in the glow of the sun,
"Let's throw it big! Come join the fun!"
Yet the snail crawls at a pace so slow,
"Party? Oh dear, I've nowhere to go!"

A butterfly flutters, tickling the air,
"Pull up your shell, don't you dare despair!
The dance floor needs your jazzy groove,
Just wiggle a bit and you'll find your move!"

With laughter ringing, the fun takes off,
As petals bop and the twigs scoff.
In every curl, there's a giggling spree,
Life's best moments are wild and free!

The Embrace of Nature's Secrets

In the garden where secrets play,
Bunnies in sunglasses dance away.
They sip on nectar, giggle and tease,
While bees try to join, but fall from the trees.

Lemons laugh as they roll on the ground,
Chasing each other, such joy they have found.
A squirrel in a turtleneck, all the rage,
Inspects a mushroom like it's on stage.

The daisies gossip, their petals all wide,
About the tall tulips and their springtime pride.
A worm in disco looks ready to shine,
Grooving to beats in the soil divine.

Nature's a jester, with tricks that confound,
Whimsical wonders in every sound.
Every corner's filled with playful delight,
In this meadow of laughs, there's no room for fright.

Stories Unfurled in the Bramble

In the thicket where tales coil and twist,
Rabbits tell stories that can't be missed.
A hedgehog types on a leaf-covered screen,
Writing great sagas from places unseen.

Berries debate on the best kind of pie,
While crickets critique with a wink and a sigh.
A fox in a fedora sips herbal tea,
As the bushes cheer, 'You're the best, yes indeed!'

Thorns wear crowns like the royalty they are,
Basking in sunlight, they shine like a star.
And snails on their journeys, so slow, yet so proud,
Share gossip of rainclouds with all of the crowd.

The bramble holds laughter in every nook,
A library of fun, just take a look.
With each rustle and giggle, a story is spun,
In this wild little realm, there's always more fun.

Stillness Under the Amethyst Sky

Under a sky dressed in purple and gloam,
Grasshoppers sing, inviting us home.
The clouds are just pillows for dreams on the fly,
While goldfish wear hats, oh my, oh my!

A turtle in shades takes his time in the sun,
Sipping on dew, he's just having such fun.
The daisies hold hands in a patchwork of glee,
Sharing tall tales of the bees' latest spree.

Pigeons in jackets strut down the main street,
Rocking their feathers, looking quite neat.
They swap silly secrets, like who wore it best,
In this lavender twilight, there's never a rest.

With laughter and giggles in nature's grand play,
Everything's funny in its own silly way.
Under the sky, where the amethyst gleams,
Life dances in rhythms that tickle our dreams.

Memories Dancing Among the Tendrils

Tendrils are twirling, what a sight to behold,
With memories spinning like stories retold.
A cat in a top hat gives wise little tips,
While mushrooms, not shy, come out with their quips.

Old leaves are doing a fancy cha-cha,
While stems clap along, "Oh, what a gala!"
The flowers are grinning, they join in the fun,
As the sun begins setting, their day's almost done.

A ladybug leads with a dazzling flair,
While ants form a line, such a stylish affair.
They dance through the garden, in rhythm and rhyme,
Creating a memory that stretches through time.

Among the tendrils, enchantments abound,
Nature's own laughter is fresh all around.
In the twists and the twirls, every being finds cheer,
In a world full of giggles, there's nothing to fear.

www.ingramcontent.com/pod-product-compliance
Lightning Source LLC
Chambersburg PA
CBHW071838160426
43209CB00003B/344